GOOGLE DRIVE AND

DOCS FOR BEGINNERS

2021

A COMPREHENSIVE GUIDE TO

MASTERING GOOGLE DRIVE AND

DOCS

DAVID B. NORRIS

Copyright

Contents

CHAPTER ONE

A Brief Introduction to Google Drive and Google Docs

Google incorporation has played a significant role in the success of many business organizations and academic fields. Google Inc has built many applications. Among these numerous applications are Google drive and Google docs. Google drive is an unconstrained data storage platform offered by Google. It allows users to create a document online and carry out any correction or re-edit it simultaneously. Google Drive also provides word processing, spreadsheets, presentation, and forms to generate online surveys and reports. To be able to use Google drive, the user must have a Google account.

This book will give you an overview of Google drive and the different applications that connect with it, the history, and its features.

Google Docs is the online representation of Microsoft word, excel, and PowerPoint. Microsoft word is called Google document; excel is known as presentation, while PowerPoint is called a spreadsheet. Google docs is a subset of Google drive because Google docs combined the characteristics of word processors, spreadsheets, and presentation programs. Google products/applications can be download by users from this link depending on their use (https://about.google/products).

What is Google Drive?

Google Drive is a safe place to store and edit your documents, spreadsheet, and slide. These documents are cloud-based because the papers' owner can invite other persons to edit and critique the file. Google Drive is a file storage system created by Google. It provides the avenue for users to store, share and edit files with other collaborators. Google Drive includes

Google docs, sheets, and slides. Google drive is of great prowess and importance to its users.

Users can access Google Drive from any platform ranging from personal computers to iPad, smartphones, and others, or logging directly into Google Drive on the web.

History of Google Drive

Google Drive is a file storage platform created by Google Inc. and launched on April 24th, 2012. The iOS app was completed in June 2012, while Google founded the Android version on February 13th, 2020. As of July 2018, it has over 1billion active users. As of December 2020, it has over 2billion users with over 3billion download globally. Google Drive offers a 15 GB free storage platform. Google also has other subscription plans, which are options ranging from 100GB to 30TB.

Features of Google Drive

Google Drive application has the following characteristics or features:

1. It has unlimited storage (15GB free storage facility).

It has other optional paid plans ranging from 100GB to 30TB, depending on the company's need.

1. It has editing capability. Users can edit and save files in the Google cloud.

2. It can share files. The owner can transfer files in Google drive with other collaborators to edit or critique.

3. Folders creation. New folders can easily be created in Google drive, whether using a smartphone or personal computer.

4. Scanning of documents. Documents available in Google drive can easily be scanned and save in Google cloud.

Importance of Google Drive

- Google drive provides backup for essential documents and files. Google Drive provides an alternative storage platform to the external hard Drive because Google drive can never be corrupt like a computer hard drive.

- Files collaboration. With Google Drive, files and documents can be sent to other persons by the re-editing and critique owner.

- Opening and editing various documents-Google Drive allows users to open documents online and re-edit on them. It saves users unnecessary stress.

CHAPTER TWO

Setting Up Google Drive

Google Drive can be accessed using a chrome browser by clicking on a new tab, or you can enter the following URL on your browser, http://drive.google.com. To access Google drive, we must first create a Google account (Gmail), but if you had an account already, continue with the sign-in.

Creating a Google Account

Creating a Gmail account is not difficult. You will have to fill -some vital information like your name, age, location, and other relevant data. After successfully creating your Google account, you can now have full access to Gmail, Google docs, Google Drive, and Google calendar. Below are the steps to create a Google account.

1. Visit the address, www.google.com

2. Click on create an account

3. Sign up form will appear

4. Accept Google terms of service and privacy policy.

5. finally, your account will be created by Google for use

How to Use a Google Drive

Google Drive is a free online storage application provided by Google Inc. it allows users to write documents online and offer the avenue to edit them simultaneously. Below are the steps to use Google drive;

- Visit the website

The first step to use Google drive is by visiting the address at (drive.google.com/drive).

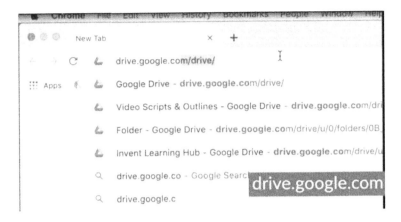

- Google drive dashboard

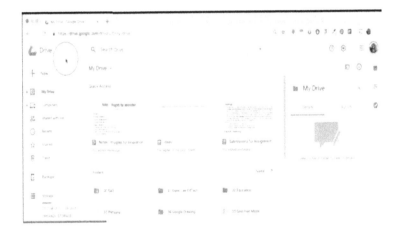

- You can create a document from the scratch

Users should create a new folder before creating a document.

Users can write the title of the paper by clicking the current

title and typing the new name.

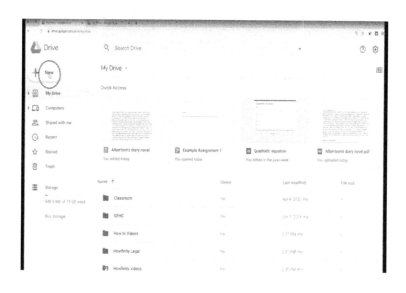

Google Drawing

Google drawing is one of the free drawing facilities embedded in Google drive. It's very similar to Microsoft Visio. With Google drawing, you can prepare organizational charts or basic drawings like shapes, icons, and images. Since Google drawing is a free web-based platform, you can get it for free without purchasing or installing it. Users can use Google drawing on more than one computer; for example, when you are drawing organizational charts at the office, but you are not through with it, you can decide to finish the drawing at home with another computer because the drawings are saved on Google drive. With Google drive, you don't need to save your drawing because it will help you save it automatically. Below are the steps to start a new Google drawing or open an existing Google drawing:

- If you want to start a new Google drawing, click the red icon in the upper left of your desktop.

- Select more and then click on Google drawings; a new window or tab will appear showing a new Google drawing page.

- If you want to open an existing Google drawing, select the graphic you wish to continue from your Google drive and then double click. Google Drive will display the picture in a new tab or browser.

You can also carry out Google drawing on your smartphones by signing to your Google drive and navigating to Google drawing and click on it. It will display on your smartphone

screen just the same way it will show on your computer
desktop.

CHAPTER THREE

Google Docs

What is Google Docs?
Google docs a free web-based software offered by Google to
complement and compete with Microsoft word. Other
services provided by goggle include sheets and slides. Google

docs are available on most devices such as personal computers and smartphones; all needed are a good internet connection and a web browser. Google docs accept different document formats such as doc, dcx, txt, rtf, and out, making it easy to view and convert Microsoft Word from Google drive directly. With Google docs, users can share files quickly, and you can collaborate with multiple persons on the same file simultaneously.

Importing a Document

After creating a Google account, as stated in chapter one, you can start creating a new document or uploading old files. If you are interested in opening an existing document like a word document, you will have to open it in Google docs first so that users can change the document format to Google Docs format. Even when you are new to Google docs, you might have some old files you want to put to use. If that is the scenario, you will have to upload all the old files before viewing and editing them. Someone can upload a document either through Google Drive or Google Docs. After uploading files, Google docs open it automatically. Then you can edit, share and collaborate with other resourced persons. To edit a document, click the blue files next to the file name from the Google docs page.

How to Check Your Spelling in Google Docs

Now that you have created new documents, you can start checking your typographical and grammatical errors to ensure everything is in place. With Google docs spelling checker, misspelled words are underlined with a squiggly line, advising you to make a change. To ensure Google drive affected the corrections, right-click the name with the line beneath, or u can press ctrl+Alt+X (Windows) or Command + Alt+X (Mac). Apart from spelling correction, Google docs come with an inbuilt dictionary and thesaurus for practical usage.

How to Collaborate with other Resourced Persons

One good thing about Google docs is the file's ability to be shared with anyone through a shareable link. The person can edit and express his view or suggestions on the document. It helps avoid sending a file back and forth between different collaborators; the collaborators can view and edit the files at once. Google docs also provide the avenue to control the power shared-users or collaborators have over the files or documents when the following options are selected:

- *Off-* this means the shareable link has been disabled. It prevents other collaborators from accessing the files. It helps in revoking the permission previously given to them.

- *Only those with the link that can edit-* the shareable links are given only to preferential collaborator to edit the files. They only have access to the file, but they cannot delete the files from your Google drive.

- ***Only those with the link can comment-*** this only provides collaborators the opportunity to comment when they desired, but they cannot edit or delete the files from Google drives.

  - ***Only those with the link can view-*** in this option, shared users can view the document but cannot view or comment on the same files.

How to Edit a Document with Collaborators

As the owner of a file and you want collaborators to help edit your files, you can access "suggestions" to allow for editing and suggestions to your documents. You are enabling permission to allow other collaborators to edit a document without the issue of them messing up the files. When collaborators are editing a file, the file owner will receive a notification email concerning the editing suggestions, which the owner file can decide to keep or reject the change.

Word and Page count

It will interest you to know that goggle docs do not display the word or page count by default. But you can quickly check them without a manual count. If you have an assignment that has to do with you keeping track of the amount you write or getting a word limit strictly, you can view everything that concerns your labors by using the word count. You can also check the number of words in the selection by highlighting text from any paragraph. You also need to know how you can view your document's word/page count; all you have to do is click Tools>word count, or press Ctrl+Shift+C on windows command+shift+c on mac. to find the word count for a specific page.

How-to-Use Google docs offline

You might be confused that since goggle docs are a web-based product, how can it be used offline? Let me ask a question in a scenario when you need your Google docs, but an internet connection is absent; what then happens? It might interest you to know that you can gain access to your Google docs offline; all you have to do is download an extension for chrome, and you should ensure beforehand you have enabled the file for offline use. When next you connect to the internet, ensure you update any changes made to the file. When you are through with downloading the official extension for chrome, by the top left corner, you will see your Google docs homepage; click on the Hamburger menu> settings. Once here, toggle "Offline" to the on position, and then you click "Ok." How then can you save storage space on your local machine? You have to know it is the most recent accessed files that Google does download and makes available for offline use. How then can you enable a file manually? In doing this, click on the three dots icon on your desktop, then go to "Available Offline" and turn it on.

Adding page numbers to a document

Page numbers are a visual tool that shows you the current page you are on. Page numbers also help you organize and place physical sheets of paper in the right order, making it easy for you to print them. Google docs do not automatically generate page numbers in files; you will have to add them manually, but it will be easier to add them to your document's header or footer. How then do you add a page number to all the pages? To do this click insert > Header & page Number > page Number>page Number. Then a window pops up from which you can choose your desired page number style.

Controlling margins in Google docs

The white space around your document at all sides is known as the margin. It will suffice you to know that you need to increase the amount of usable space on the space whenever you reduce the margin size. The reason for the above is because margin creates an invisible border. If you so desire to increase or decrease the amount of space on the edges of all of the File's pages, all you have to do is manage its margins by using the ruler along the side and at the top of the document. There is another option available to you, which is you entering the margins manually. To do this, click File> page Setup, enter the number of white spaces you wish to see on each side, then click "OK."

Adding a textbox to a document

Adding a textbox to a document is not straightforward because it is unlikely from the drawing feature. In Google docs, adding text boxes is crucial because it helps you highlight important information and get you abreast with specific document elements. In adding a text, we mentioned the drawing feature, and to do this, you need to access the drawing menu. In accessing the drawing menu, all you need to do is to go to Insert>Drawing and click the text box icon in the menu bar. Then you will click and hold your mouse to create a textbox in the provided space, after which you add your preferred text. When done with that, you click on "Save & Close" to insert the textbox into your document when you are through.

Adding a table of contents

A table of content gives readers a view of each topic/chapter listed in a document. Automatically this feature generates one and uses links that take you to each section when you click on it. It helps you access specific parts when you have larger documents, saving you the stress of strolling through the wholes document. In doing this, you click Insert>Table of contents, and you then click on one of the two options provided. The choice that appears first is a plain-text table of contents with numbers on the right side for ease of printing of documents. The second option is the one that has to do with you inserting a hyperlink that takes you to the noted section to view documents online; it must suffice you to know that this second option does not make use of page numbers. In creating an automatically generated table of contents linked to specific sections of your document, you will have to use Google docs' built-in header styles in formatting each of the chapters or title. You making use of Google docs enable docs to know how it will add clickable links and populate the table.

The preferable Google docs add-on

Having been abreast with Google docs' basics tools and knowledge will be vital to know add-ons because it will make you a real power user. Add-ons are more or less like extensions for web browsers it enables you to access additional features from third-party developers. You can increase productivity using other proofreaders, an in-document translator, a rubric creator for teachers, and even a document signing the app. All these features can be done by installing the tools.

CHAPTER FOUR

Google sheets

What is a Google sheet?

Google sheets are slowly becoming the best spreadsheet choice for thousands of people since it is easier to collaborate in Google's sheets than other spreadsheet tools. New features and functionalities are frequently updated to make things get done efficiently and faster.

Google sheets are a web-based spreadsheet application that helps you store and organize numerous types of information, just like Microsoft excel. Google sheets are also a programmed used for creating and editing spreadsheets.

Google sheets, Google docs, and Google slides are all parts of what Google calls Google drives. Google sheets make it easy for those who have modest spreadsheet requirements, work remotely from more than one device, and collaborate with others. Google sheet is an online app that you can use anywhere, nothing like I forgot my spreadsheet files at home. It works from any device, with mobile apps for iOS and android alongside its web-based core app. Google sheets is a powerful tool because it is all you expect from a spreadsheet, with the extra perks of an online app.

How to Create a spreadsheets

In creating a spreadsheet, you can use an office suite, or you can make use of software like excel; the spreadsheet works more or less like excel, and it can be of great use when you have an important spreadsheet you are ben tasked with.

I will take you through some steps on how you can create a spreadsheet:

1. You will need to sign in to Google sheets. To do this, you need to visit docs.google.com/spreadsheets, after which you

sign in either with your Gmail or your Google account is your choice.

2. You need to view your existing sheets. When you have logged in, the spreadsheet will take you to the main directory. If you had an existing spreadsheet before, you could view and access your spreadsheets from here.

3. You will need to create new/fresh spreadsheets.

In this place, you will have to click on the large red circle, which has a plus sign in the lower right corner. Then you will open a new tab or window with the web-based spreadsheet.

4. You need to give the spreadsheet a name. There appears an "untitled spreadsheet" and is said to be the current name of the spreadsheets on the top left corner. All you need to do is for you to click on it, and then you will see a small window. Type in the name you want to give to the spreadsheet here, after which you will click on the "OK" button. Then the name will start reflecting.

5. The next thing to do is to work on the spreadsheet. Like the way you work on Microsoft excel, you can work on your Google sheets in the same way. You will come across the header menu and a toolbar with functions like those of Microsoft excel. It is pertinent to know that you don't have to save with Google sheets. The reason is that everything has automatically been saved at regular intervals.

6. The last but not least is for you to exit the spreadsheet when you are through. When done with your current document, you can close the window or tab, and everything has automatically been saved. You can make use of Google sheets or Google drive in gaining access to your document.

How to share, protect and move your data

Sharing of data can be done with your friends, a colleague, or anyone who has gotten an email address either from their mobile app or from the web. All you have to is to follow the under-listed steps:

Step 1. Click on share

You have to open the file you wish to share, then go to your web browser and click on the Share button located by the upper right corner. When you are editing with your mobile app, click on the horizontal dots on iOS, while on your android device, you click on the vertical dots, then it is usually a three-dots menu. Then you click on share and export in the upper right, and then you click on share.

Step 2. Adding people

you will need to enter each individual's email address you will like to share your work with. When you enter a portion of someone's name in your Google contacts or your organization, the system will display potential matches you need to select.

Step 3. Adjusting of roles

This step is optional and not so compulsory to follow. Just by default, everyone you added will all be accessible to your work as an editor; this implies that they will be able to make changes to your document. But you have left with the choice of decreasing this access they have to that of a commenter, enabling people to add and respond to comments that have to do with the file, or viewer, which gives access but does not allow comments and changes. Since your web browser or Android mobile app, tap the pencil icon, select can edit, can Comment, or can View. While in your iOS mobile app, select the pencil icon, click Editor, tap Commenter, and lastly, tap Viewer.

Step 4. Adding message

This step is optional and not a must-use step by everyone; people who use adding messages wish to put down a little message explaining why they had shared a document with someone.

Step 5. To send

The last step is to send the sharing invitation. To do this, you can either click on the icon that looks similar to a paper airplane icon and iOS mobile apps or click on send on the web. To be able to share data; one can also import data from another spreadsheet. In sharing your data, all you need to do is to open the file you want to share, click on share, enter the email addresses or groups you want to share with, then choose what access you want to give to people, either editor, commenter, or viewer, then click on send.

Haven is known how to share your data, how do you secure this data. Even though you shared your data internally or externally, you may wish to stop someone from accidentally tampering or overwriting your data. Suppose you want to prevent someone from deleting your formulas or information. In that case, you need to secure your data. In protecting your data, it can be locking your data in the worksheet structure or setting a password.

To lock your data in Google sheets, you have to do the following;

- It would help if you opened a spreadsheet in Google sheets.

- The next step is to click on data. Protected sheets and ranges.

- Then Click adds a sheet or range, click range.

- Then you will need to click on set permissions or change permissions.

- Then you will have to choose how you want to limit editing.

- Lastly, Click save or done.

How then can you set a password in securing your data?

Setting a password helps prevent people from tampering with your data and making changes to it. To set a password, you need to indicate the worksheet you wish to protect; then, you move to your tool menu and click on protection, then select protect the sheet, then the program will come up with an option asking you which specific part of the worksheet do you wish to protect; after doing that when you select a password, then click on the OK button, the program will then ask you to enter, re-enter the password, then the last thing is to click on the OK button.

Now you have understood how to protect your data, how then can you move this data? Excel helps you move information from a cell to another cell, meaning no need for you to type the data into a new cell and then erase the data from the location it was before. In moving your data, firstly, select the cells you intend to move. Secondly, click on the selected cells' border, then drag the cells to the location in the worksheet where you intend to move the data. Lastly, observe that excel has moved your data.

The collaboration of documents with others

Collaboration makes it easier for you to keep track with your co-editors and see the changes that were made and who made these changes. Collaboration can make your work easier. In collaborating with others, you can adapt the email approach by clicking on the file, then you add a subject and a message then you send.

Data formatting and adding formulas

In formatting your data, you use the print, undo/redo, the font setting/styling function icon, and the shortcut key, just like what you have in your word processor.

In formatting your data, you have to do the following;

- At first, you have to open a spreadsheet in the Google sheets app.

- Afterward, you tap a cell, and then you drag the blue marker to the cell you which to use.

- Then you click on format.

- Then go to the text tab choose an option to format your text bold.

- In the cell, tab choose an option to format your cell

- Lastly, you tap on the sheet you want to make use of in saving your changes.

Adding of formulas

Regarding adding formulas, the word formula and function have always been used interchangeably, especially when it relates to spreadsheets. Formulas are being seen as simple operating tools, just like cell A2+ cell B2, for example. You have to click on the cell where you wish to place the formula. Then you tap on the formula or enter text to make the keyboard display. Then type=sum (to start the formula. Choose the numbers you want to add together.

Some Google sheets formulas you can make use of are listed and explained below;

the trim formula- most times, when you go to your spreadsheet, and you open up your data, it does not look clean and neat at all times; there appear to space most of the time.no need to panic in this kind of scenario; all you need to do is to make use of the trim method because it helps to bring your work to a normal shape by cleaning up those trailing and leading spaces that appear in your work. The trim method saves you the stress of

- By clicking on each cell to clean them up instead, trim automate them for you. How then can you apply this trim formula? To make use of Trim, type =TRIM, and then direct your cursor to the cell you wish to clean up; after doing that, you click on enter, then you tidy all the data at a fast pace. Whenever you have data with spaces that you desire to remove, always have this formula at heart.

- The Proper formula-in the same light of cleaning up data, at times, it appears your data came out unusually just like the lowercase and uppercase format. When it appears like that, you need to use the proper formula to save you the stress of typing your data from the beginning again; it also helps transform your text to the title format. How can you make use of the proper formula? All you need to do is type = PROPER, and then direct your cursor to the cell you wish to clean up. Then click on enter, you will notice some changes in your work's capitalization and will then match the proper style. Always know that you can pull the Google sheets formula downwards to make it reflect on all the adjacent cells.

- The GOOGLE FINANCE FORMULA- the goggle finance formula is a lifesaver to all those who wish to track their stock portfolio. It is a formula that goes directly to Google's financial data store, which provides you with information regarding stocks, mutual funds, ETFs, and others. This formula can help you pull so many different kinds of data points about security, and there appears a basic usage to pull the latest price of General Electric Company:

=GOOGLE FINANCE ("GE", "price")

Google finance will pull and keep up to date General Electric stock price right inside of a spreadsheet. To track your portfolio values, you can apply this formula.

With the help of Google Finance you can get data on bonds, stocks, and funds directly from the service.

THE =GOOGLE TRANSLATE FORMULA- in making fast translations of your data, you should apply Google Translate services. But it's preferable when you make use of it directly inside a spreadsheet. Take, for instance, you downloaded data from systems that bring out text in an international language. You will have to translate it repeatedly whenever you get new data, and you drop it into your spreadsheet. Just make use of the =GOOGLETRANSLATE formula inside your spreadsheet to save you the stress of going forward and backward to the Google Translate website and constantly copying and pasting data between both.

The easiest way to make use of this formula is simple for you to type.

=GOOGLE TRANSLATE (A2), e.g., to take it to cell A2 with text is broken down in a simpler form. Google will decide to dictate the language and help your account in providing your default language.

Similar to the GOOGLE FINANCE function, the GOOGLE TRANSLATE function is a simple illustration of Google web-based spreadsheet tool's supremacy. It's not difficult to apply to your spreadsheet data. It is attached in the prowess of Google other services

RANDBETWEEN

In creating my spreadsheet exercises, one of the tools that are of great importance to me or serve me better is the usage of the RANDBETWEEN function because it helps generate values bit by bit (randomly) used in exercises.

To make use of =RANDBETWEEN, what you do is to easily open up the function, in which to be followed is the provision of a lower and an upper limit for the value.

Using Google sheets offline

Though google sheets' primary function is to create and edit spreadsheets while you are online, you can also gain access to it when you are also offline; how does it work? Its works by creating local copies of your files to gain access to it when you are in an environment where connectivity is sparse or when you are in a cellular dead zone. It would be best to have Google chrome, Google drive chrome web app, or even Google drive sync. There are some steps listed below on how to gain access to Google sheets offline and also how we can gain access to a spreadsheet without connection.

- Open Google sheets.

- You will have to click on the menu icon after you have logged into Google.

- The next step is for you to select settings.

- Then Click on turn on. If it has been turned on before, you may have enabled this feature while making Google docs available offline.

- You will then click on get the app.

- Then Click on add to chrome

- Then Click on add extension

- Then Click on the Google sheets tab.

- Then Click on enable offline. Your docs will then start to download for offline accessibility and ensure you don't disconnect immediately because the process takes some time.

- Finally, when you lose your internet connection, you have to open Google Sheets and then click on one of your documents. For your convenience, you have to bookmark the page.

Removing duplicates

One of the common things people do in Google sheets is removing duplicates. Below are some steps you need to get abreast on removing duplicates from a data set in Google sheets.

Firstly, you have to select the dataset from which you want to remove the duplicate records. You need to click on the data option from the menu.

Secondly, click on the remove duplicate option.

Thirdly, in the remove duplicate dialog box, ensure Data header row is selected (in case your Data has the header row).

Fourthly, ensure all is selected (in the columns to Analyze section)

Lastly, click on the remove duplicates button.

When done with the above steps, all duplicates will instantly get deleted from the dataset, and you will get your desired results. Making use of remove duplicates does not tamper with your rows or cells; it only deletes the duplicate records from the cells (without interrupting cells around the dataset).

Adding comments on Google sheets

To further your collaboration with others, you need to add comments to your Google sheet which will help you get feedback, offer suggestions, and tag contacts in a comment. The following steps will guide you on how you can add comments to your Google sheets.

Step 1. The first step is to the right click on a cell and selects Insert Comment. You can also make use of your shortcut keys which is ctrl+Alt+M for windows or you make use of Cmd+Alt+Mac.

Step 2. The very next step is for you to tag your contacts and you can do this by making use of the @ or + key to enable a list of your contacts to pop up, then you can select the numbers of contacts you would love to make use of or allow to comment.

Step 3. When you are done entering your text and tagging your contacts, all you have to do is click on a comment. Mind you tagging a contact in a comment will not distort the settings used for sharing. Ensure you assign the right access in the share settings to enable someone to view or edit the documents

CHAPTER FIVE

Google slides

It must suffice us to know what a Google slide is all about. Google slides are seen as a presentation program included as part of the free web-based Google docs editors suite that Google offers. This Google slide offers services such as Google docs, Google sheets, and Google slides. It is pertinent for you to know that Google slides make your work outstanding due to presentation themes, hundreds of fonts, and embedded videos. Google slides also said to be a presentation app that is usually used online, which helps you create and format presentations and enables you to work with other persons. Google slides are not only a presentation tool that allows you to make offline presentations. It also helps you make offline presentations.

Having been acquitted with what Google slides is all about; let's discuss how to create presentations.

Creating a presentation

I will enlighten you with some steps in creating a presentation.

- You need to go to the Google home page, and then you click on the grid towards the upper right-hand corner. Afterward, you click on the drive icon. When done with that, it will take you to a login page if it appears that you were signed out; otherwise, it will be directed to your drive. You can as well type https://slides.google.com, which will direct you to the slides page.

- Go to your drive and click on the blue new button on the left side of the page. Afterward, you click on "Google slides" from the drop-down menu. To get more options, go through the arrow on the right edge of the Google slides option, then you will see a smaller drop-down menu; you can then proceed from here in creating a presentation either from a blank slide or from a template.

- Go to the slides page if you are presently not there, but if you are there already, select an option from the top of the page in creating a new slide. When searching for blank slides, you can click on one of the templates available should in case you don't like the templates available, you can get more templates by clicking on the template gallery option, or you can click on the white square that has a plus sign with it.

- You will need to give your slide a name, and you also have to select a theme. In selecting a theme, you will need to make use of the "luxe" theme. For you to be able to give it a name, you need to click on the "untitled text on the top to give it the name of your choice. After giving it your preferred name, that name will then start reflecting in the browser bar when you view your presentation or when it has been viewed by someone else. Please ensure a title and subtitle are added, and you do this by clicking where you were asked to add text.

- You will need to add new slides. You will come across a small+button at the upper left corner; all you need to do is click on it to create the default title and the body slide. If you are not satisfied with this approach, you can also adopt another approach. All you will need to do is to click on the small down arrow right next to it. Where it will take you to a large drop-down menu of many different layouts for different purposes; if you wish to change a slide layout that has been in existence before, you can successfully do that by clicking on the layout option on the existing upper bar.

- You need to insert an image. In inserting an image, all you need to do is go to the upper editing bar, and you click on insert; afterward, you look for images in the drop-down menu. A window with different image options will immediately come up. You can search for your picture online either with Google, life or stock images, you can also search for your picture from a drive, you can search for a photo from your Google photo album, you can also paste an image URL, you can upload your image from your PC (personal computer), or you can take a picture from your webcam.

- The next thing to do is for you to add text. If you don't have an open space with a "click to add text" prompt, you will have to click on the box with a T in the upper editing bar. You can make some changes to your text size; even your text fonts are either you making your text bold, underlined, or getting even italicize.

- You can even italicize your text; these options are all next to each other; you can also edit your texts with line spacing, indents, and alignments; you can also use numbers and bullets, which I made use of in the course of this work. Instead of using numbers, I used bullets, which are those black circles you can see.

- The next step is what we call animate. For this, you will have to right-click text. Please don't left-click text if you won't be doing the right thing; as I said right-click on text or a picture, most preferred is the one you wish to animate first. You are to make sure that whatever it is that you have selected must be highlighted in blue. Then you will see a rectangular shape that says fade-in; as we all know, this is the default animation. Then you will have to make use of the drop-down menu in selecting an animation. You can also decide how you want your animation to be automatic or manual; in doing this; you will come across a different rectangle title. All you need to do is click on this, and you will get your desired result. It is very pertinent for you to know that for bulleted lists are compulsory you animate by paragraph. You can also decide on each animation's speed limit; you can do this by dragging the bar. To add animations to each element, you need to click on the blue `+ after doing that, and you need to select the object you wish to animate; after doing this, they will all begin piling up, then you will have to click on them one after the Other for you to edit. After doing this, you will have to change the transition, and it should be done from slide to slide, to do this all you need to do is click on the default "slide: No transition" at the top of the sidebar. The decision is left for you to decide if you want to apply on just one or all the slides. If you wish to see the animations you have done, all you need to do is click on a play at the sidebar's bottom. You can also remove your animation by clicking on the small x on its rectangle, and then you change which order you want it either up or down by dragging each animation to the direction you want.

- If you are done editing, the next thing to do is for you to edit how to grant permission for your presentation. to do this you will have to find the persons you will like to share your presentation with, you can search for this persons either with their names or through their email, after doing this you will have to change permission by clicking the pencil icon next to it, is either they view, edit or comment on it. It is so crucial for you to know that clicking on the button gives you a presentation link that is so special to you and can access it by clicking "Get shareable link". When you are through, click on done.

- The last step is to view all the things you have been doing since which we call the finished product. For you to see your work all you need to do is click "present" on the upper right-hand corner, then you navigate from slide to slide in navigating from slide to slide you make use of the arrow keys or the arrows at the bottom of the screen. After that you turn on the laser pointer by clicking on the squiggle at the bottom, then for a full-screen view, you have to click on the four outreaching arrows, name of the current slide to change to another, and make use of the gear for settings. It would then help if you got feedback from your audience questions and answers and special notes, which is done by turning on the presenter view.

Importing a Microsoft PowerPoint presentation

In importing your PowerPoint presentation, we are going to make use of the visme comparison alternative. All you need to do is import your existing PowerPoint presentation into visme, and you will edit and present them into visme presentation software. After which to make your work more presentable, you will have to spice up your slide design with visme. The following steps are how you can import your PowerPoint presentation, whether old or new.

1. Since we are making use of visme, you have to log into your visme dashboard. Your visme dashboard contains all your existing projects, and also you can create new projects here.

2. You have to locate the import icon and click on it. You might be confused on how the import icon looks like, and it's the grey button which is right next to + Create towards the left sidebar. To enable the upload comes up click on it.

3. You will have to upload your PowerPoint file. When you are done clicking the import icon, a write up comes up asking you to upload your presentation. After which you will have to choose your PowerPoint file from your PC (personal computer) to do this, you will click on the browse file button and then click open to let the import process begin.

4. Editing your PowerPoint. When you are done importing your PowerPoint presentation, you will see it on your visme dashboard with your other project. You can use Visme's design elements such as stock photos, icons, maps, charts, graphs, and others in editing your slides.

5. Sharing your PowerPoint offline. Importing your PowerPoint is so important because it enables you to share and present your PowerPoint online. With the help of visme, you are left with the option of generating a shareable link in the course of your presentation, and you can embed your presentation on a blog post or webpage.

Collaborate and share presentations

Collaborating and sharing your presentations make others gain access to your work and to do this you have to do the following;

Firstly, when you want to collaborate, click on share in the top-right corner of the ribbon.

Secondly, select the email addresses or names you would like to share your presentation with. You can as well choose the drop-down to change your permissions. Allow editing is normally checked by default, if you wish for you to view permission only, then uncheck this box and click on apply.

Thirdly, if you like you can add a message after adding a message, you click on send. This is all you need to know about collaborating and sharing your presentation.

How to make templates on Google slides

You have to be aware that your Google slides template presentation tells more about your work to your viewers. You can make, design and create templates on your Google slides. Let's see some ways on how you can make templates on Google slides.

Firstly, you need to open your Google drive, and to do this you have to input this word in the Address field of your browser https://drive.goggle.com.after doing that, your Google drive gets opened. When your Google drive is opened, then you need to create a new Google slides presentation. Then in the upper left, you will see the new button click on it. From your drop-down menu, you click on Google slides then an empty presentation comes up. You will have to give your presentation a new name of your choice for you to identify your work easily. To rename it type a new title in the upper left and that is all.

Secondly, you have to create a master slide. Some ways on how to create a master slide are discussed below;

- Choose Slide> Edit master title from your main menu: you can also change the font of your presentation with just a click on the text placeholder on the master slide and selecting it. The word Arial is what was used in defining your current font.

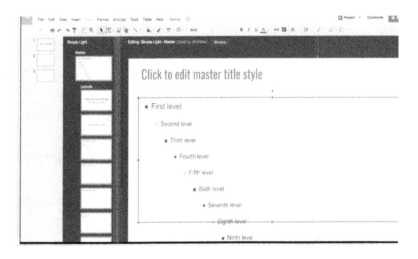

- The next thing to do is add a graphic element to your Google slide template, in the course of this work, we will add a logo. In adding a logo all you need to do is click on the master slide, beneath the main menu you will come across the toolbar then you have to insert image icon from the toolbar then the insert image dialogue box shows up.

The next thing to do is to download an image from your PC, all you need to do is to click on the choose an image to upload button in other for you to download an image from your PC when you are through with that you have to drag the image to where you desire to save it on your Slide.

Thirdly, the third step is adding master layouts. Within your master slide tool, you can start adding your master layouts by clicking on (Slide > Edit Master). You can also delete extra layout by deleting any recent master layouts you don't want to make use of any more to select it by clicking on it after which you right-click. The next thing is to select the delete layout option, which will show up from the menu. When you are done discarding those master layouts that are not of use to you, you can make changes to those leftover templates to match your preferred layout design.

Fourthly, how can you use the new Google slides template that you have created? When done creating your template, then it is ready to be used. How then can you use it? You have to get a copy of the template by inputting File > Make a copy option on the main menu. The next thing is to give the copy the desired name of your choice. The next thing is to make duplicates of the copy you will need, and this is done by right-clicking on your preferred sample slides. It can be one or two or even more then use the Copy command from the pop-up menu. The next thing is to place the slides in the way you want them to appear in your presentation, click on each slide and place them in the right manner. The next thing is to input your information into the presentation. After doing that you can add the image, you will like to make use of in your presentation. These are some of the crucial things you need to know on how to make templates on your Google slides, please you are to follow the steps one after the other to give you a good outcome.

CHAPTER SIX

Google photos

A Google photo that was evolved or established by Google is described as a means of sharing pictures and being a depot for other Google products and services.

Google photo is the domicile in which your photos and videos could be orderly arranged for ease of sharing. Google photos are among the most desired apps used in backing up your photos, organizing your photos and also used to share in sharing your photos. Making use of Google photos is easy to use and not hard because it is straightforward. When you have uploaded some of your pictures into Google photos, then the next thing you need to do is to keep them organized, in keeping them organized what you have to do is to create different albums which you can use to group all your pictures. Be rest assured that your photos are safe, secured, and private to you.

Creating a new album

Creating an album in Google photos is so easy, and it helps you organize your photos into a special group. You can make use of a mobile app in creating an album, or you can create an album in Google photos. Be abreast with the fact that in creating an album in Google photos it can either be done on your desktop and mobile. Firstly, I will show you how you can create an album in Google photos on your desktop. Some of the steps on how you can create an album in Google photos on the desktop are as follows:

Step 1. You have to log in to your Google account, in doing this just type in https://photos.goggle.com.

Step 2. you will come across the word "ALBUM" click on it, after clicking on it you will see a plus (+) with blue color above the words "create album" click on it.

Step 3. You need to give your new album a name to click on "Add photos" and then click "select from your computer" to choose the photos you wish to add.

Step 4. You have to click on "Done."

When you are done with all these steps, you can share your new album with other persons, but it is your choice to decide.

Having been enlightened on how you can create an album in Google photos on desktops, let's go through how you can create an album in Google photos on your mobile. The following are the steps on how you can create an album in Google photos on mobile.

How does a Google photo work?

Step 1. You need to download the Google app on any browsing phone you have at your disposal be it an android phone or an iPhone. Then you sign in to your Google account.

Step 2. At the bottom of the screen, click "Albums" after doing that click on the plus (+) sign with blue color inside the "New album" box.

Step 3. Type in the name of an album and click on "Add photos" and select the preferable image you will like to make use of from your camera roll.

Step 4. when you add an image, click on the little back arrow at the screen's top left. You can also decide to share the new album if you decide to, it is your choice.

You need to know you can gain access to your album at anywhere you signed in to your Google account using Google photos. Whether the album was created from your computer or on your mobile device doesn't matter.

Creating a shared album

The following are the ways on how you can create a shared album on Google photos;

- You have to go to your computer and type in the keywords photos.google.com.

- Go to your Google account and sign in.

- By the left menu, click on the photos present.

- Select and click on each video or photo you desire to share.

- Create appears at the top click on it

- You have to give your album a title.

- You have to share your album when you are done with everything to click on share.

- The last thing is to determine the people who will gain access to your album.

It must suffice you to know that with your Google account you can share your album directly to anybody you wish to share it with provided they appear in your contacts, or you can search by making use of their phone number you can as well search with their email address. If you wish to make it accessible to everyone, you can create a link to share it. Be aware that you will send a link to the people you shared your albums or photos with and any individual who has access to this shared link can automatically view the photos or albums you shared.

Being acquitted with how Google photos work can help you optimize your photo storage, independent of whatever device you are using. Google photos enable users to upload new images, view latest photos, edit new images, save and create new videos, collages, animations, photos, books and albums. You can as well download all the things you wish to download. That is to say, and your cloud-based backup can back up itself with ease on your external hard Drive and also your computer. With an android device, you can reduce your backup data usage, to avoid being short of data when you start uploading things in the background. You can also preserve a copy of your photos and videos for yourself by setting your Google drive, to do this you go to your Drive's settings, turn on

"Create a Google Photos Folder," then you save. Google photo is a vital tool that is also versatile. That needs just a slight effort from you. After all, you don't need to go through the stress of thinking about the storage for your photos and even the storage that you need to provide your video with good quality, Google photos settles them all because it gives you unlimited storage. It is the best option for those who wish to back up their media files. With an Android or iOS device, you can make use of Google photos. With Google images, be rest assured that your work's media is automatically backed-up. Google photos not only help you to store, share, view, and edit your videos and pictures, and it also helps you manage your media with an Al-powered assistant being given to you. You can opt to back up your photos and videos automatically just the way you took them to those persons without a Google device. To share your albums and pictures with ease, all you need to do is use the share feature, not minding if there are photos. All you need to do is ensure the "backup and sync" feature is turned on; it will be interesting to know that you can still retrieve all your files deleted from your trash about 60 days ago. You can make your photos searchable within your account even though you have archived the images to get them out of the way. Google photos help users with more auto-generated extras like the grouping of pictures together based on some factors such as date, people, and the places featured. It also helps in creating phone book collections. The users are also provided with an option to print or ship their books. With the assistant supplied to them, it can take photos captured in rapid succession and make them be GIFs, also known as "animations."

What will the user gain when they make use of Google photos?

There are numerous things users can gain when they use Google photos because it can be frustrating when you are repeatedly running out of storage on your smartphone. And people face these challenges since some smartphone cameras can be of high quality, and we know as humans we love photos, but this photo consumes a lot of space on our device. But the good news is that Google photos are a freeway in providing solutions to these drop backs irrespective of the device you are making use of; it can be an iPhone or an android phone. Just navigate to photos.goggle.com. You can only do this when you have signed in to your Gmail account, meaning you must have a Gmail account; if you don't have one, you will need to sign up for one; signing up is easy and free. Then you can start using Google photos. When users use Google photos, they can automatically share as many of their pictures they have uploaded with their loved ones, friends, and so on. Users can also decide which of their unique photos should be auto-shared either by date or topics. With all these benefits, including unlimited storage, it must suffice me to say Google photos have become the most preferred option for managing an extensive media library. An added advantage is that it is very convenient.

Notwithstanding, another benefit of Google photos among users is that it serves to store, share, view, and edit photos and videos. In addition to this is the inclusion of an Al-powered assistant to help in managing your media. I am merely saying that it will automatically help create albums, videos, and stories from your photos. It adds music to your movies, which can manually be edited for further polishing.

Google photos do provide an automatic backup for your media with unlimited storage space.

Conclusion

Google photos are of great importance because they take your photo library entirely and upload it to the internet.

Google photos are secured to an extent, but it doesn't post your pictures for everyone to see automatically unless you share them with others.

Therefore, we could say then that the benefits ascribed from the use of Google photos by users cannot be oversized as Google photos are a safe home for lifetime memories.

Google drive and Google docs form part of Google suite of productivity and collaboration tools. With all which has been said above, the confusion between the two subjects is understandable.

Gaining access to Google drive and Google docs is the creation of a free Google account.

The benefits users' gains through the usage of Google drive are the use of a straightforward interface, compatibility of

Microsoft office, easy access to documents no matter where you are designated, and other Google docs advantages. Documents are the foundation or building blocks of any business; this is to suffice that Google docs' importance cannot be over-emphasized.

Google developed Google photos, and it's a photo-sharing and storage service. It was released in the year 2015 which is now hugely popular nationwide. Google photos do have apps for iOS and Android, in addition to it is the presence of a web.

ABOUT THE AUTHOR

David B. Norris is an international technology analyst born in New Jersey, in America. He specializes in computer education and career advancement in the area of Google services. He also aims at meeting special educational needs on informational technology.

He has experience in graphic designing, and mentoring a team on Google drive and docs. He also has extensive experience in computer software and applications.

Made in the USA
Las Vegas, NV
01 March 2023

68344033R00046